By

Phillip Rich

EKKLISIA PROPHETIC APOSTOLIC MINISTRIES, INC.

Published By Ekklisia Ministries

Copyright 2012

All rights reserved under International Copyright law. No part of this publication may be reproduced, stored in a retrieval system, or transmitted, in whole or in part, in any form or by any means, electronic, mechanical, photocopying, recording or otherwise, without the prior express consent of the publisher. All scripture is the Kings James Version unless otherwise stated. All rights reserved.

Take note that the name satan is not capitalized. We choose not to acknowledge him, even to the point of violating grammatical rules

TABLE OF CONTENTS

Introduction 1

The Name of the Lord is a Strong Tower . 13

Zoe Life in Him 28

How to Enter Into His Name 37

~ In His Name~

Introduction

I want to show you that religion has tried to do things from the flesh to the spirit when we are supposed to be operating from the spirit to the flesh. You can't bring lasting change by trying to do it in the natural realm. Anything that is going to be lasting, have rewards, have blessings attached to it has to start from the spirit and bring change to the natural. Everything we know has its roots in the spirit realm, both good and bad. We can put band aids on anything we want to, but unless we get to the root we will never see permanent change.

There is great power in the name of Jesus when you are in the name. We are going to look in the Word to see how many times we are told to do something in His name. Then we will also look at how important it is, describe how important it is and why some people will speak the name of Jesus and not see something happen.

~ In His Name~

Did you know that the name of Jesus is not a magical name? It is a powerful name, but not magical. There are people who speak it and have no results. There are others who will whisper it and changes take place all around them. I want to share with you how to enter into the power of that name.

Mark 16:17,18; "And these signs shall follow them that believe; In my name shall they cast out devils; they will speak with new tongues; they will take up serpents; and if they drink anything deadly, it will by no means hurt them; they will lay hands on the sick, and they will recover.

Acts 19:13-16; "Then certain of the vagabond Jews, exorcists, took upon them to call over them which had evil spirits the name of the Lord Jesus, saying, We adjure you by Jesus whom Paul preacheth. And there were seven sons of one Sceva, a Jew, and chief of the priests, which did so. And the evil spirit answered and said, Jesus I know, and Paul I know; but who are ye? And the man in whom the evil spirit was leaped on them, and overcame them, and prevailed against them, so

that they fled out of that house naked and wounded."

These people were using the name of Jesus like it was a magical name. A lot of Christians are doing that and not seeing the results.

There is tremendous power in the name of Jesus and that is the point. It is in the name. I want to give you three very powerful truths about in the name and show you that there is a place in the name where you can speak it with such high levels of authority that the demonic spirits know who you are. We need to understand that they have to know who you are in Christ before they will listen to what you have to say. In other words, we have to come into Him.

A Place

Let's look at the words "in the name". The Greek word for in is *en*[1] and actually means a fixed position, a place. It is a place in God.

There is a place in Jesus, a cleft in the rock, a secret place.

---

[1] #1722 in Strongs Concordance

~ In His Name~

Psalms 91:1; "He that dwelleth [takes up residence] **in the secret place of the most High shall abide under the shadow** [the authority covering] **of the Almighty."**

Remember authority trickles down. It has to be given to you by someone you are under subjection to. Otherwise, you are getting that authority illegally and that is called usurping authority. Satan tried to usurp authority when he said he wanted to be like God. He wanted to take a position that didn't belong to him. When it comes to authority in God, it has to be delegated.

Some people have no right to use the name even though they are Christians. They are not in God, are not under the shadow or the covering of the authority of God. They are not obedient to God, not walking with God, not living right. They are not living for Jesus. It is important that we come to the place where we live for Him. He is to be our life. We are to come into Him.

Colossians 3:2-3; "Set your affection on things above, not on things on the earth. For ye are dead, and your life is hid with Christ in God."

~ In His Name~

You die out to self in order to live unto God and to live in Him.

Psalms 91:9; "Because thou hast made the LORD, which is my refuge, even the most High, thy habitation;"

Some have the Lord come into them as Savior, but when they come into Him then He truly becomes their Lord, their covering. They are hidden in Him. When the devil gets a look at them, he sees Jesus because they are in Him. Their life is hid in Christ.

Intimacy

Psalms 91:14; "Because he hath set his love upon me, therefore will I deliver him: I will set him on high, because he hath known my name."

Known is a word of intimacy. The Hebrew word is *yada`* (*yaw-dah'*) meaning intimate with. Some people are not intimate with Jesus so they have no right to use His name. There is no power when they speak His name because they don't really know Him. There is an intimacy with God that takes you to high authority. When you are intimate with God then you have all the rights that

God has and they are bestowed upon you because you are one with Him.

When the bible says that Adam knew his wife, it was not a "*Hi, wife. Glad to know you.*" It was intimacy. We could say it was *in-to-me-see*. In other words, you become so intimate that you open your heart and tell the Lord what you are feeling, what you are going through. The Lord opens His heart and tells you how much He loves you and what He wants to do in you. You look into each other's heart. You are eye to eye with Him.

2 Corinthians 3:18; "But we all, with open face beholding as in a glass the glory of the Lord, are changed into the same image from glory to glory, even as by the Spirit of the Lord."

Open face means without the veil. Without the veil means we have entered the inner chamber of intimacy with our groom. We are the bride and have taken off the veil because we are in the inner chamber with Almighty God. In this place of intimacy the bible says we are changed from glory to glory. That means there are different realms of glory. Every time I am intimate with God I am changing more into His image, into His likeness. I am carrying more of His authority. It is not our authority, but His authority delegated unto man. He gives everything to those with whom He is intimate.

In a marriage contract, the husband endows all, including all his worldly goods and his name, to his bride. That is why the wife takes on the name of her husband. It is all tied into intimacy with God. When we are intimate, married to Him we take on His name. That means we have legal authority to go into the bank and sign the same name, we are in the family. God's bank account belongs to us because we are married. All His authority is ours because we are married.

To Come Into

The third part of "in the name" means to come into His nature, to come into His character and personality in order to come into His authority.

Some people don't act like Jesus, but they still want the power of Jesus. It won't happen. The demons know who has His nature, that means who really have His name. Name and nature mean the same thing. Sickness knows who is in His name. Poverty and lack know who is in His name. Even the elements of this world know who is in His name.

Ephesians 5:1; "Be ye therefore followers of God, as dear children;"

The Greek word for followers is *mimetes* (*mim-ay-tace'*). It means one who is an imitator or the exact representation of.

We know that in New Testament times they began to call people Christians. Do you know why? It was not because they were following Christ, but because they were acting like Jesus. They carried His nature, His likeness, His personality so much that when the world looked at them they were called Christians. The word Christian means Christ-like or an exact representation. In other words we become like Him because we see Him as He is. You can't see Him as He is without intimacy. He unveils all to us in intimacy.

Nobody knows me as well as my wife does. She knows my human side, knows things that others would never know. I let her know all about me because of intimacy, of relationship. She carries my name and the authority that I carry. It is delegated to her. She can go to the store, buy whatever she wants and sign my last name for it. When we are in a church service and the Holy Ghost speaks to her, she doesn't have to ask me if it is okay because I have already told her that she knows how to hear God so go ahead and write the check. Now she can run it by me for confirmation, but I trust her and know she hears God. There is a connection of intimacy.

Ephesians 5:8; "For ye were sometimes darkness, but now are ye light in the Lord: walk as children of light:"

You have to walk out the Word, do what God's Word says. You are children of light, so act like it, talk like it and walk like it.

Ephesians 5:9; "(For the fruit of the Spirit is in all goodness and righteousness and truth;)"

This is what the name of Jesus is all about – the nature, the character of God and the fruit of the Spirit.

Ephesians 5:10-11; "Proving what is acceptable unto the Lord. And have no fellowship with the

unfruitful works of darkness, but rather reprove them."

Unfruitful means barren works. They don't produce in your life. If it is not producing, then the Lord is not in it. Only what can produce life is of God. That includes ministry. What is of God has life, fruit.

We are not to have fellowship, intimacy with darkness. We are supposed to be children of light, having fellowship with light, with God and His people. That will always produce fruit, produce blessing. Any relationship not producing fruit that is a blessing is not a godly relationship. A God relationship benefits everybody. When God starts connecting hearts, everybody is blessed. It is never one sided.

Ephesians 5:13; "But all things that are reproved are made manifest by the light: for whatsoever doth make manifest is light."

In other words, anything that produces is light. If it produces life, then light did it. If death comes out of it, then darkness was its author.

~ In His Name~

God is connecting us with Himself and with His people. Out of it will come higher dimensions of God. If the people you are running around with do not take you to another level, then it is time to get connected to somebody else who is on fire for God and pressing on toward Him. You can tell when someone has been with Jesus.

There is a place in Him where you don't even have to say His name because you are already in His name. Jesus never used His own name to cast out devils and we are supposed to be one with Him. Lester Sumrall didn't go around using the name of Jesus to cast out devils. There is nothing wrong with it and he used it occasionally. There were many times he would walk up to someone who was possessed, command the demons to come out and they left. When asked why he didn't use the name of Jesus, Lester said it was because he was in the name. He would go on to say that his very life and existence screamed out the name of Jesus.

One of my earlier pastors traveled with A.A. Alan. In one of the tent meetings there was a woman who was possessed by devils. They had to chain her to a post in the tent. Those type of individuals would be dealt with after the service.

~ In His Name~

About thirty bible school students went over to this woman and began screaming the name of Jesus at her and hitting her with their bibles. She was throwing these men around as if they were rag dolls. This went on for a couple of hours when Bro. Alan finally decided he needed to do something about it. He walked over, knelt down by the woman, whispered in her ear and immediately all the devils came out of her. My pastor went up to Bro. Allen and asked what he had said to that woman. *"Devil, this is A.A. Alan. You had better come out now."*

Until you understand what "in the name" is, you will think that is all wrong. I believe in using the name of Jesus, but only if I am in the name. Otherwise I am no different from the seven sons of Sceva who were trying to use the name as a magical name without the authority of it.

~ In His Name ~

The Name of the Lord is a Strong Tower

Proverbs 18:10; "The name of the LORD is a strong tower: the righteous runneth into it, and is safe."

Mark 16:17; "And these signs shall follow them that believe; <u>In my name</u> shall they cast out devils; they shall speak with new tongues;"

This verse in Mark does not say we will be speaking the name, though that is inferred. That inference is not what it is really saying.

In the last chapter we shared a little about the seven sons of Sceva from Acts 19. They tried to cast out demons using the name of Jesus. The demons said they knew Jesus, knew Paul, but asked who the seven sons were. We said that the name of Jesus is not a magic name, though it is a powerful one for those who run into it. Jesus said in His name we would cast out devils, not by using His name.

We also shared the meaning of "in my name". "In" is a fixed position in God. "Name" means to be intimate with God, with His nature, His character, His personality and ultimately with His authority.

We come into a fixed position in God.

Psalms 91:1; "He that dwelleth in the secret place of the most High shall abide under the shadow of the Almighty."

That secret place is being in the name.

Intimacy with God is the next part. Intimacy always brings communion. If you are intimate with God then you are joined to Him and everything He has becomes yours. That includes His authority and the use of His name. Through marriage the wife takes on the name of the man she is joined to. We take on the name of the Lord when we come into Him. Many Christians are not married to the Lord. They want Him to be their savior, but are not allowing Him to be the Lord, the groom. They are not coming into Him, not running into the name and are not in the name. When you are married to someone you are committed, sold out. You do not belong to yourself anymore. You belong to that person and that person belongs to you. This is how you come into the name. This is how you are able to cast out devils. Jesus said "in my name you will cast out devils." He did not say by using His name or by His name.

Mark 16:1; "They shall take up serpents; and if they drink any deadly thing, it shall not hurt them; they shall lay hands on the sick, and they shall recover."

These things are also available to those who are in the name. They can lay hands on the sick and the sick will recover because they are in the name. The name of the Lord is a strong tower and the righteous run into it. In the name is where the power of the name is. It is only in the name where we have power. The Lord made it very plain that His name is not a magical name. His name is power, but only for those who are in it.

In Acts 4, the religious leaders told the disciples not to teach in Jesus' name because when they started teaching in His name power went everywhere. It wasn't just teaching or teaching the name of Jesus, though they did that. The disciples were in His name, in a relationship and it brought great power.

Acts 4:17-18; "But that it spread no further among the people, let us straitly threaten them, that they speak henceforth to no man in this name. And they called them, and commanded them not to speak at all nor teach in the name of Jesus."

Those religious people never sent for the seven sons of Sceva to tell them not to say the name of Jesus again. In fact Jesus was a common name in that day. Every time a parent called their son Jesus to come in, the demons didn't tremble or people get healed.

We have to understand the power of coming into who He is. That is the power of the name. The power of the name is in the name. Come into the name and power will be there. It will be available for you.

I speak the name of Jesus, but it is only going to be powerful for me as I am in the name.

~ In His Name~

The religious leaders did not tell the disciples not to speak the name of Jesus. They were told not to speak or teach in His name.

The Lord showed me that if what I believe is not bringing forth results then there is something I am not believing correctly. If the doctrine I have is not producing, then I am missing some revelation. It is like hooking up a sound system and all the wires have to be just right. If one wire is not hooked up right, it will not work. It is the same way with our relationship with God. We have to get all the wires connected, get everything put together. How will we know when it we get it right? It will work. There are results.

There is answered prayer if we are in His name. If we abide in Him and His words abide in us, then we can ask what we will and it shall be done. Coming into Him, partnering with Him, being married to Him are being in the name.

Something happens when you have a group of believers coming into the name at the same time.

~ In His Name ~

Matthew 18:20; "For where two or three are gathered together in my name, there am I in the midst of them."

We know we are in the name when we look like Him, talk like Him, take on His character, act like Him and do what He did. We will automatically take on His authority.

Midst in the Greek is *mesos* (*mes'-os*). It means being in the middle of. The Lord is in the midst of us, among us, accompanying us, in the middle of us manifesting who He is both spiritually and physically. This is talking about a glory so awesome that the priests could not stand to minister because of the glory of God that filled the house.

If we want the glory of God to come in a service, we have to come in His name. Unforgiveness, disagreements, bitterness, resentment, insecurity, backbiting, jealousy are not in His name because they are not His nature, character or likeness. So to come into Him we have to lose who we are, lose our own identity, our own personality. We are supposed to be taking on His personality. When we come into the name we won't have all the quirks of our personality. We won't have any excuses because we are supposed to act like Him and not like us. The scripture says as He is so are we in this world.[2]

We are being transformed out of who we are into who He is, from glory to glory even as by the Spirit of the Lord. We are being changed into the same image, the same nature, the same personality by the Spirit of God. So we can't use excuses anymore for our temper or temperament. If you are going to be a follower of Christ, you will be an exact representation of your master Jesus. It cannot be done by your flesh, but by your spirit which is transformed when you come into His name. You are transformed every time you look into His face in intimacy. You are changed into more of Him until eventually you don't recognize yourself anymore. When you look into the mirror you will see Jesus in your own eyes.

When you grasp this you will understand why those prayers weren't answered, why the devil didn't move when you rebuked him and the disease didn't do anything when you rebuked it. It means you were not into Him enough. There is a constant level to level, from grace to grace, from

---

[2] 1 John 4:17

glory to glory of coming into Him. I am coming into Him every day, more than yesterday. Every day I love Him more. Every day there is a new dimension I am coming into and I am being transformed by it. I am not going to be the same anymore.

The Exalted Name

Mark 16:17; "And these signs shall follow them that believe; In my name shall they cast out devils…"

Notice, He didn't say by His name or by speaking His name. He said in His name. There is a difference.

When you come into the name, then you come into the power of the name. You can't speak the power of the name without being it. Blessed is he who cometh in the name of the Lord.

Proverbs 18:10; "The name of the LORD is a strong tower: the righteous runneth <u>into</u> it, and is safe."

Safe, delivered or set free. This verse doesn't say the righteous just use the name of the

~ In His Name~

Lord. They run into it. Speaking the name is included, inferred, but that is not the point of the scripture. You have to run into, come into God.

Many have had the Lord come into them and that is a start. But don't stop there or you will remain immature. The Bible says if any man be in Christ he is a new creature.[3] In Christ is different from Christ coming into you.

Christ in you, the hope of glory means you have heaven as your home when He comes into you. But when you come into Him, you come into heaven now and you experience authority on levels you only dreamed of before. You can have everything you read in the Word if you abide "in me". Abide means to dwell, to come into God. Some people are not getting anything because they are not in God. It is time to come into God.

I want to share some things with you about the name.

Matthew 28:18-19; "And Jesus came and spake unto them, saying, <u>All power is given unto me in heaven and in earth.</u> Go ye therefore, and teach

---

[3] 2 Corinthians 5:17

~ In His Name~

all nations, baptizing them in the name of the Father, and of the Son, and of the Holy Ghost:"

What kind of power is in heaven? It is the power of the Father, the power of the Holy Ghost and Sonship power. The power of the Trinity has been given unto Jesus. We have to know that first in order to understand the power of coming into the name.

Jesus said all power had been given unto Him. Then He said to go baptize in the name of the Father and of the Son and of the Holy Ghost.

Power means authority. Authority in the Greek is *exousia* (*ex-oo-see'-ah*). In our verse it means the judicial, supreme authority has been given unto Him in heaven and on earth. Then Jesus goes on to tell the disciples to teach and baptize.

The name of Jesus embodies all the names of God and that why it is so powerful when we come into it. It is the name of the authority of the Godhead. When you speak the name of Jesus you are saying Father. When you speak the name of Jesus you are saying Holy Ghost. When you speak the name of Jesus you are saying the Son. When you come into Jesus you are coming into all three, not just one of the Godhead. You can't come into Jesus without coming into the Father or the Holy Ghost. It is impossible because they are one.

Did you know there is another name for Jesus?

Isaiah 9:6; "For unto us a child is born, unto us a son is given: and the government shall be upon his shoulder: and his name shall be called <u>Wonderful, Counsellor, The mighty God, The everlasting Father, The Prince of Peace</u>."

Jesus is called the everlasting Father in Isaiah.

Philippians 2:6-9; "Who, being in the form of God, thought it not robbery to be equal with God: But made himself of no reputation, and took upon him the form of a servant, and was made in the likeness of men: And being found in fashion as a man, he humbled himself, and became obedient unto death, even the death of the cross. Wherefore God also hath highly exalted him, and given him a name which is above every [all names that are named] name:"

~ In His Name~

All the names include all the names of God. They are included in the name of Jesus.

Colossians 1:19; "For it pleased the Father that in him [Jesus] **should all fullness** [completeness] **dwell;"**

Colossians 2:9-10; "For in him [Jesus] **dwelleth all the fulness of the Godhead bodily. And ye are complete in him, which is the head of all principality and power:"**

The Father, Son and Holy Ghost (the Godhead) are wrapped up in Jesus. In Jesus is everything, including the Godhead bodily. When you come into Jesus you get the Father. When you come into Jesus you get the Holy Ghost. You get all three. In Him is the fullness of the Godhead bodily. Jesus is the head of all principality and power. In other words, He is over everything including the demons and the devil. Do you understand how powerful your Jesus is?

Ephesians 3:12; "In whom [Him] **we have boldness and access with confidence by the faith of him."**

~ In His Name~

When you come into God you will be bold and will have access to everything God has with confidence. When you come into Him demons will be no problem. When you come into Him, sickness and disease has to go.

Several years ago I had an associate pastor who called me one Sunday morning to say he was too sick to get out of bed. He wanted me to come and pray for him. As I started out the door I heard the Lord say, *"All you have to do is go and sit on the edge of the bed."* I walked in the bedroom and sat on the edge of the bed. As soon as I did the associate pastor said he wasn't sick anymore. He got up and got ready for church.

There is a place in Him where demons know who you are because of who you are in. That is why the devil didn't know who the seven sons of Sceva were. The Lord wants us to move into that place. He is calling us to Himself so we will come into the name, come into Him, into the fullness of the authority and all that He is, the completeness of God. You will come into the one who has all the government of the entire universe upon His shoulders.

~ In His Name~

1 John 4:17; "Herein is our love made perfect, that we may have boldness in the day of judgment: because <u>as he is, so are we</u> in this world."

There is a place in God where this verse becomes your verse, where you can say of yourself *"As He is so am I in this world. I dwell in the One who carries the government of the entire universe upon His shoulders. In Him I live, move and have my being."*

There is a place in God and God wants us to move into it. We have been satisfied too long with only having God in us. Thank God that He is in us. It makes heaven our home. But when you come into Him you come into heaven, the authority, the fullness of who He is now. You will be like Peter, walking around and everybody gets healed. Peter never said a word. Read Acts 5, two multitudes got healed when Peter walked by.

Peter came into God. Talk about change! When you come into Him all things become new. You won't have any more excuses of age, hair color, race, nationality, ancestors or where you come from. When you come into Him the old passes away and all things become new.

~ In His Name~

2 Corinthians 5:17; "Therefore <u>if any man be in Christ</u>, he is a new creature: old things are passed away; behold, all things are become new."

Christ is in many Christians, but they are not in Christ. When you come into Christ things change. You become different because you belong totally to Him. You will live differently, act differently, talk differently, think differently and see things differently. Your perspective will be different. People who come around you will know something is different.

Many years ago an evangelist friend of mine came so into the Lord that when he just walked to the mailbox, people would fall over healed when they walked past him. Why did this happen? It was because he came into the name of God.

Proverbs 18:10; "<u>The name of the LORD is a strong tower</u>: the righteous runneth into it, and is safe [full, healed delivered, full of the completeness of God, of complete authority]."

~ In His Name~

Zoe Life in Him

Acts 1:1 talks about the things that Jesus both began to do and to teach. There is a time when He confirms the Word with signs following. The signs may follow the Word you preach or there may be a confirmation of that Word before you preach. There were times when Jesus would do something to get someone's attention and then He would teach the Word. Signs and wonders were used to get their attention so they would believe what He said.

Mark 16:20; "And they went forth, and preached every where, the Lord working with them, and confirming the word with signs following. Amen."

It is scriptural to have the manifestations before or after the preaching and teaching as long as you understand that with the things of God there should always be some form of confirmation.

~ In His Name~

Called to Minister?

I want to share some prophetic insight for those who feel God has called you to some form of ministry or you might be called upon to teach, preach or share in some sort of way.

I have learned over the years that you have to pray and wait on God for the Word to preach. Did you know you also have to pray and wait on God for the confirmation? There are two things I do. I pray and wait on God until He gives me a scripture that bubbles up in my spirit while I am reading and in the Word. I will study what He gives me and a message will come out of it.

Some will stop there and go preach the Word, but they will notice that usually nothing takes place afterwards. There would be no signs, wonders, manifestations or at least not to the level they desire. The reason is because they didn't wait on God for the manifestation the same way they waited on God for the Word.

I also spend time asking God to show me things in the spirit about people, reveal anything He would want me to say or do. I pray for manifestations to take place and for Him to give

~ In His Name~

me words of knowledge, words of wisdom, discerning of spirits. I pray that God will move in a particular way. I wait on God for Him to confirm His Word. I spend time pressing in, waiting on Him for things like that. A lot of times He will begin to give me direction and I will write it down.

The mighty men of God from the days of tent meetings did this all the time, but some of them didn't pass it on to other ministries. Maybe they didn't know how to so they died with those secrets. There were mighty moves, but they didn't continue. Now people have to pick up on these things in the spirit and begin to share them.

The fivefold are equippers. I am not going to win the entire world by myself and be a great evangelist. Neither will you. You can join hands with other people and together with other believers shake the world for Jesus Christ. With his whole life of evangelism and with the mighty crusades he has done, Billy Graham has not reached the whole world. Neither did Oral Roberts.

Reaching the world will not just happen with one doing it. We must connect with each other. We must share secrets and not be jealous of one another. It is not our ministry, but the ministry of Jesus Christ to the whole earth.

In God we join hands with one another. You are only as powerful as the people you connect and interconnect with. Never forget that. When you start networking with others and joining hands with others, you will accomplish so much in the kingdom of God. You become like the company you keep. Run with the wise and you become wise. Run with fools and you will be destroyed. [4] You must connect, join hands and together we will shake and change the world for Jesus Christ.

Zoe Life

God is bringing us into Him, into the fullness of who He is. When you come into God you lose yourself.

Colossians 3:3; "For ye are dead, and your life is hid with Christ in God."

Galatians 2:20; "I am crucified with Christ: nevertheless I live; yet not I, but Christ liveth in me: and the life which I now live in the flesh I

---

[4] Proverbs 13:20

live by the faith of the Son of God, who loved me, and gave himself for me."

It is important that we know we are in Him. In Him we live, move and have our being. It is time to come into Him. When you come into God you find out what life is all about.

John 1:4; "In him was life; and the life was the light of men."

Until you come into God you don't know zoe life. The zoe life is the abundant life that God lives. You don't know what abundance is, what abundant living is all about until you come into Him.

There is a difference between having Jesus in your heart and being in God. He wants us to come into Him.

Colossians 2:6-7; "As ye have therefore received Christ Jesus the Lord, so <u>walk ye in him</u>: Rooted and built up in him, and stablished in the faith, as ye have been taught, abounding therein with thanksgiving."

~ In His Name~

Do you really want to grow, be established, mature? Then come into Him and you will be rooted, established and built up in Him.

When you come into God you can minister to others. When you are not in Him, you always want to be ministered to. Even though we all need ministry, we need to come to the place where we can minister to others and be a blessing.

In Him there is a place of complete confidence, even in your prayers.

1 John 5:14-15; "And this is the confidence that we have in him, that, if we ask any thing according to his will, he heareth us: And if we know that he hear us, whatsoever we ask, we know that we have the petitions that we desired of him."

When you come into Him you know that whatever you ask in His name, according to His will, you know He hears you. If you know He hears you, then you know you have the petition that you have desired of Him. In Him you will ask according to His will. In Him is where prayers are answered.

~ In His Name~

In Christ is the same thing as in Him.

1 Corinthians 1:30; "But of him are ye in Christ Jesus, who of God is made unto us wisdom, and righteousness, and sanctification, and redemption:"

When we come into Him, we get His wisdom, His sanctification, His righteousness and come into full redemption.

Many have not gone deep enough in God. They have accepted Him as savior, but don't know Him as Lord. When He is your savior He comes into you. When He is your Lord, you come into Him. There is a difference.

You can tell when a Christian has not come into Christ because the authority level is not there. The glory is not on them. They don't act like Jesus, look like Jesus or do anything Jesus did. These people just have a ticket to heaven and that is great. What about a destiny to do something in the earth so we can take souls with us? You have to come into God to do that.

Ephesians 1:3; "Blessed be the God and Father of our Lord Jesus Christ, who hath <u>blessed us</u>

~ In His Name~

<u>with all spiritual blessings</u> in heavenly places <u>in Christ:</u>"

It is in Christ that all these spiritual blessings are given to us. When you are saved, those blessings belong to you, but only when you come into Him do you actually get them, see the manifestation of those spiritual blessings.

John 15:5 says that when we come into Him we begin to bear fruit. In other words your life will be fruitful. You will be a fruitful vine and your life will produce something. Others will see the glory of God on you and they will experience it.

John 15:5; "I am the vine, ye are the branches: <u>He that abideth in me, and I in him</u>, the same bringeth forth much fruit: for without me ye can do nothing."

It takes both abiding in Him and Him abiding in you to bear fruit. We are to come into the fullness of who He is and let our lives be hid in Him. We need to be locked up in Him.

Colossians 2:10; "And ye are complete in him, which is the head of all principality and power:"

~ In His Name~

Complete means full of supply. You have all you need when you come into Him.

Coming into God is an ongoing thing. I am going to be pushing for the rest of my life to fully come into Him. There are depths, levels, things in God that those of us who are in God have just touched on. There is so much more in Him, no way to tell the depths of Him. The further in God you go, the more of Him you get. The more manifestations, blessings you get. You can get lost in Him the more of His personality, nature and character you get. You will be lost in Him, but truly found.

In Him we live. In Him we move. In Him we have our being. Isn't He awesome and wonderful?

~ In His Name~

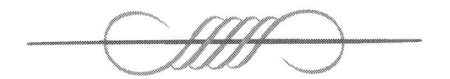

How to Enter Into His Name

Jesus didn't command us to speak His name and cast out devils. He said to come into His name and in His name we shall cast out devils. In His name we shall lay hands on the sick and they will recover.

Acts 17:28; "For in Him we live, and move, and have our being…"

When you come into God, you come into all that He is. We are nobody when we are not in Him. The devils didn't know the seven sons of Sceva because they were not in God.

In His name, in Him, in whom and in Christ are all the same term. They all talk about coming into God.

Colossians 3:3; "For ye are dead, and your life is hid with Christ in God."

~ In His Name~

It is in God that we have all that we have.

I want to share with you four things that the bible says about how to come into God. The name of the Lord is a strong tower that the righteous can run into and be saved. We have to understand how important it is that we come into His name. We must also understand the power of it as well as the how to. I believe in practical Christianity. I don't believe in just having a doctrine that is not practical. It needs to be workable theology that is practical, down to earth and you can walk it out. We need simple truths revealed in such a way that we can implement them.

Dwell in Him

John 6:48-56; "I am that bread of life. Your fathers did eat manna in the wilderness, and are dead. This is the bread which cometh down from heaven, that a man may eat thereof, and not die. I am the living bread which came down from heaven: if any man eat of this bread, he shall live for ever: and the bread that I will give is my flesh, which I will give for the life of the world. The Jews therefore strove among themselves, saying, How can this man give us his flesh to eat? Then Jesus said unto them,

~ In His Name~

Verily, verily, I say unto you, Except ye eat the flesh of the Son of man, and drink his blood, ye have no life in you. Whoso eateth my flesh, and drinketh my blood, hath eternal life; and I will raise him up at the last day. For my flesh is meat indeed, and my blood is drink indeed. He that eateth my flesh, and drinketh my blood, <u>dwelleth in me, and I in him</u>."

Dwelleth is *meno* (*men'-o*) and literally it means to continue in Him, to stay in Him, to remain in Him, to come into a given state of abiding.

We have to eat of His flesh and drink of His blood, then we will dwell in Him.

The Greek tense for the words eat and drink mean to eat and to keep eating, to drink and to keep drinking. They are verbs with an ongoing action. We have to eat and keep eating, drink and keep drinking.

Let me explain to you what Jesus meant. He is the bread of life. His Word is also called bread.

Matthew 4:4; "But he answered and said, It is written, Man shall not live by bread alone, but

~ In His Name~

by every word (rhema) **that proceedeth out of the mouth of God."**

The Word of God is what you need to eat. Man can't live by eating natural bread only. We need to eat spiritual bread.

Jesus was saying in John 6 that His flesh is bread and His bread is the Word of God that is going to feed the hungry. When we eat of His flesh we are eating of the revelation of the Word, the rhema. The written word can't feed you by itself. It has to be germinated, made alive by the Spirit of God through your prayer and waiting on Almighty God. When you wait on God He turns the written Word into a rhema. In other words, He gives you fresh baked bread. You must eat and keep eating the revelation of the Word of God. A revelation a day keeps the devil away, keeps sickness away, keeps poverty and lack away. You need a fresh revelation every day. You have not eaten until you have had revelation.

If we eat three meals a day, how much should we be eating in the spirit? We are supposed to eat of His flesh which means to eat and keep eating of His flesh, the revelation of the Word.

~ In His Name~

You need to read the Word, but not just to be reading it. Don't read it so that you can tell everybody that you read through the Bible fourteen times this year. That is a flesh thing and you will not enter the revelation of the Word. What you have to do is get into prayer and get in the Word. Let the Holy Ghost lead you and as you read something will come alive out of the Word. When the Holy Ghost starts germinating that Word, starts making that fresh baked bread stop and eat it. Don't move on to something that is not fresh bread. Get a concordance out. Look at other scriptures that talk about it. Study that thing out and meditate on it. Mediate means to chew on. Chew on it until you get all of the goodness out of it. You may be chewing on it all day, getting all you can out of that bread. Your life will change as you do. You are being nourished and are coming into Him.

Jesus also said we must drink of His blood. Leviticus 17 talks about the life of the flesh being in the blood.[5] Life in that verse means the spirit. Life and spirit are the same in the Word of God. The life of the flesh is in the blood tells me that spiritual power is in the blood. So when you drink

---

[5] Leviticus 17: 11 and 14.

in of the blood, you are drinking in of His Spirit. When you worship, sing, sing in the Holy Ghost, are loving on Jesus and His presence starts to fill the room drink it in because you are drinking of the blood.

When we eat of His flesh and drink of His blood we dwell in Him. We come into God when we eat on a regular basis and keep on eating, drink and keep on drinking. Keep eating the revelation and drinking of His spirit and you will come into Him. You will be dead and your life will be hid with Christ.

Keep His Commandments

1 John 3:24; "And he that keepeth his commandments (the commandments of God) **dwelleth in him, and he in him. And hereby we know that he abideth in us, by the Spirit which he hath given us."**

Notice it says he that keepeth. The word keepeth (*tereo, tay-reh'-o*) is a military term. It means to guard over, to fulfill it, to know it is a command from your superior and it must be done.

~ In His Name~

He that keepeth the word means to follow the command, to guard over the command from your superior and you must fulfill it because you are under obligation. He is your commander and you are under authority. When you keep you come into Him. You dwell and abide in Him.

When you come into God by keeping His commandments you can ask what you will and it shall be done.

There are all kinds of benefits for coming into God, including power in prayer. There are people who pray and are not in Him. Their prayer is a maybe, hope so, think so, hit and miss. Then there are people who pray and heaven moves to the earth. It is not a hit or miss thing because they are in Him. If we abide in Him and His words abide in us, it shall be done. Shall means impossible not to happen.

Walk in Love

1 John 4:16; "And we have known and believed the love that God hath to us. God is love; and he that dwelleth in love dwelleth in God, and God in him."

~ In His Name~

1 John 2:9-11; "He that saith he is in the light, and hateth his brother, is in darkness even until now. He that loveth his brother abideth in the light, and there is none occasion of stumbling in him. But he that hateth his brother is in darkness, and walketh in darkness, and knoweth not whither he goeth, because that darkness hath blinded his eyes."

We may say we love our God, but hate our brother. How can we say we love someone we cannot see, when we cannot love someone we can see. Do you know what the word hate means? It doesn't mean to despise, but to love less than yourself.

We actually hate someone when we don't love them as much as we love ourselves. Our love level isn't as high as we think. It takes that love to come into Him. You have to love others more than you love yourself to come into the true love of God.

We have to start walking a love walk.

1 John 3:17; "But whoso hath this world's good, and seeth his brother have need, and

shutteth up his bowels of compassion from him, how dwelleth the love of God in him?"

If we can't care for the people we see, how can we say we care for God? I must want to pour my heart out to you. I must want to release what is important to me into you. I must be willing to give time, prayer and release myself to your life to say that I love you. Otherwise it is meaningless words. When there is true love, you will come into God. When you come into God everybody will know it.

1 John 2:6; "He that saith he abideth in him ought himself also so to walk, even as he walked."

We have to start walking this thing out. We cannot call ourselves Christians if we are not living it. You can't come into God only by what you believe unless what you believe is what you do.

Be a Follower

There are two Anglo-Saxon words that make up the word belief. The first part is "be" meaning to live or exist. The next part is "lyfan" and means in accordance. In other words, to live or exist is accordance with. The Greek word for belief means to say something based on what you believe. The Hebrew word is to do something. When James said that faith without works is dead, he was speaking as a Jew to other Jews, Greeks and Gentiles. He was reminding the Jews and explaining to the Greeks if you say you believe, but don't do then you don't believe.

Look back at 1 John 2:6. *"I am in God. I am abiding in God. I have come into God."* If that is true, then walk as Jesus walked. When you study the word walk you will find it means to live, to be occupied with, to have a life style. A walk is what you do every day. It is the path you trod daily. We should do what Jesus would do. It is not the doctrine that is in my head, but my lifestyle that is in my walk. It is my walk that brings me into Him and keeps me in Him. If I want to stay in Him, this has to be my lifestyle. It cannot just be a doctrine or belief system. It has to be an action, my lifestyle. I am a Christian which means Christ like, an exact representation of.

Ephesians 5:1; "Be ye therefore followers of God, as dear children;"

Followers means imitators of or an exact representation of. We are to be like Him. We are

~ In His Name~

His offspring, His children. We are to walk as He walked, live as He lived. When you do, you come into God. When you come into God things start changing. Jesus never lived with a day of defeat. He never lived with an area that He didn't know what to do with. Jesus always went to His Father and spent time in prayer. He always had an answer no matter what the enemy would do, no matter what the circumstances were. He always knew what to do.

Jesus had problems on the earth. People despised, rejected and spoke evil of Him. He faced storms and problems. People would start out walking with Him and turn around and leave. When He spoke of eating His flesh and drinking His blood a multitude left Him and so did the seventy. We never read that the seventy came back. They didn't take time to find out what He meant. When you know somebody you don't jump to conclusions.

If I were to say something that was a bit off the wall, hard to understand and you knew me, you would come and ask me what I meant by that. Others who are really trying to find fault anyway will accuse me and walk out the door.

~ In His Name~

The Bible says that the disciples came to Jesus and asked Him to explain what He had said. He asked if they were going to leave Him also. They responded by asking where else they could go to find words of eternal life. They knew He was the Christ.

In conclusion, God wants us to live our lives wrapped up in Him. Not only is He to be resident in us, dwelling and directing our daily lives, but we are to come into Him. As we come unto the revelation of His Word and who He is and we learn to abide in prayer and in His presence we will find all the benefits of the Word of God will work more readily and completely to the full manifestation of the results that we read about in the Word of God. When we are in Him demons WILL flee, diseases WILL be healed, those we minister to WILL be set free and our prayers WILL be answered. This is what it means to come into and live in His name.

Made in the USA
Columbia, SC
30 April 2025